Travel Through Time
On the Road

Road Travel Past and Present

Jane Shuter

Raintree

Chicago, Illinois

For more information address the publisher:
Raintree, 100 N. LaSalle, Suite 1200, Chicago IL
60602

Printed and bound in China by South China
Printing Company.

08 07 06 05 04
10 9 8 7 6 5 4 3 2 1

Library of Congress Cataloging-in-Publication
Data

Shuter, Jane.
  On the road : road travel past and present / Jane
Shuter.
      p. cm. -- (Travel through time)
Includes bibliographical references and index.
Contents: Travel by road -- Getting moving --
Empire building -- Pulled by horses -- Paved roads
-- First cars -- Early car journeys -- Mass
production -- Public transport -- Road revolution -
- Trucks -- Different worlds -- Roads in the future.
  ISBN 1-4109-0582-9 (hc) 1-4109-0981-6 (pb)
 1. Roads--History--Juvenile literature. 2.
Transportation, Automotive--History--Juvenile
literature. [1. Roads--History. 2. Transportation--
History.] I. Title. II.Series: Shuter, Jane. Travel
through time.
  TE15.S58 2004
  625.7--dc21

                    2003010202

Acknowledgments
The publishers would like to thank the following
for permission to reproduce photographs:p. 4
Ashmolean Museum; p. 5 Photodisc; pp. 6, 16,
21 Hulton Archive; pp. 7, 12 Peter Newark's
American Pictures; p. 8 John Seely; pp. 9, 13, 20
Bridgeman Art Library; p. 10 Lee Snider/Corbis;
pp. 11, 28, 29 Corbis; pp. 14, 15 Mary Evans
Picture Library; p. 17 Topham Picturepoint; pp.
18, 26 Popperfoto; p. 19 Robert Harding Picture
Library; p. 22 Advertising Archive; p. 23 Alamy
Images; p. 24 Sally and Richard Greenhill; p. 25
Ted Spiegel/Corbis; p. 27 Roger Ressmeyer/Corbis.

Cover photograph of a U.S. car advertisement
from 1928 reproduced with permission of
Advertising Archive.

Contents

Any words appearing in bold, **like this,** are explained in the Glossary.

From Tracks to Trucks

The first people on the earth had to walk to get around. They used the same ways over and over, making tracks that they could follow. These tracks were often hard to travel on in bad weather because they soon got muddy and slippery, or covered over in snow.

NOMADS

The earliest people moved from place to place searching for food, following the same paths each year. Some peoples then settled in one place and grew their own food. Others, called nomads, still traveled the old roads, looking for food.

This is a model of the type of cart that early nomads would have used to carry their tents and belongings in.

Trade happens when **goods** are swapped for different goods or money. When people began to settle and trade between villages, traders wanted to carry as many goods as possible. By 5000 B.C.E. people were using animals to travel and to carry goods. They also **invented** all kinds of vehicles for animals to pull.

Modern travel

People now travel mainly on roads in vehicles. Goods are carried in trucks. The vehicles can go very fast, depending on the road speed limits, and how much traffic is on the road.

Modern roads are very busy. Traffic can crawl along slower than walking speed.

Getting Moving

The earliest vehicle scientists know of is the **sleigh,** used from about 5000 B.C.E. In about 3500 BCE people in **Mesopotamia invented** the wheel and used animals to pull carts.

From earliest times, Plains Indians in the United States used a **travois,** which was light and easily pulled over flat grassland by horses or dogs.

All kinds of wheels

Mesopotamian carts had solid wooden wheels. They were strong and went over bumps without breaking. They were heavy, though, and slowed the vehicle. When other peoples used the wheel they changed it to suit their needs. Ancient Egyptian **chariots** and carts from the Siberian plains both had lighter wheels, which could move easily through sand and grass.

Rules of the road

By 1000 B.C.E. the ancient Chinese had many roads. They were used by people on foot, people riding animals, or carts pulled by animals. They had rules about the size of vehicles, how fast they could go, and what to do at road **intersections.** Officials made sure everyone followed the rules.

LAND AND WEATHER

Different vehicles worked well in different countries. Sleighs were best over even ground and in places where it snowed. Where the ground was bumpy, people had more reason to invent wheels.

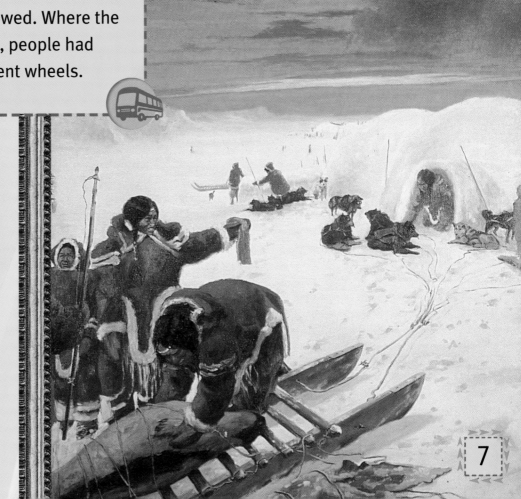

Sleighs may have been the earliest vehicles. They have been used all through the past in snowy places.

Empire Building

In about 500 B.C.E. the city of Rome, Italy, began to take over more and more land around it. By about 260 B.C.E. the Romans controlled most of Italy. They kept taking over more and more land, building an **empire.**

This Roman road is in Pompeii, Italy. The stepping stones are for people to cross the street and are the right width apart for carts to go through the gaps.

As the Roman Empire grew it needed to move soldiers, **settlers,** and **goods** farther and farther. Good roads were very important. By C.E. 400, Roman roads stretched for about 56,000 miles (90,000 kilometers) in all directions from Rome. They were as straight as possible, to take the shortest route.

Who built the roads?

The army built the first roads in the Roman Empire. Each section of the army had its own **engineers** to tell the soldiers what to do. These roads were then repaired, and sometimes made wider by local workers. An ordinary traveler could cover about 50 miles (80 kilometers) a day on a Roman road.

As the Roman Empire and its soldiers spread to new lands, more and more roads were built.

BUILDING ROMAN ROADS

Roman roads were made by digging a trench. They flattened the soil at the bottom, then added a layer of sand, which was smoothed down. Next, they put a layer of big stones and covered it with cement. Then a layer of small stones, sand, and cement went down. The final layer was of big, flat stones.

Paved Roads

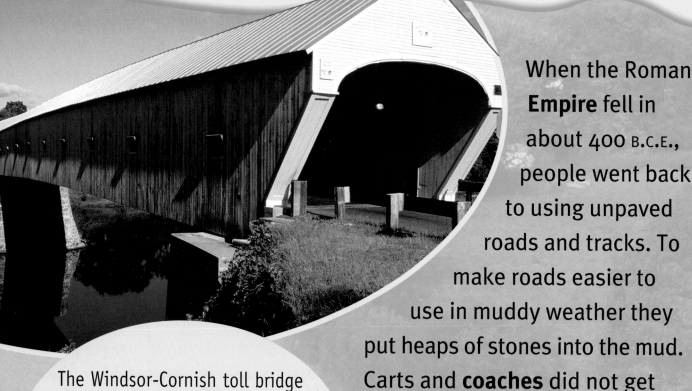

When the Roman **Empire** fell in about 400 B.C.E., people went back to using unpaved roads and tracks. To make roads easier to use in muddy weather they put heaps of stones into the mud. Carts and **coaches** did not get stuck in the mud, but their wheels did get caught between stones instead.

The Windsor-Cornish toll bridge in the United States opened in 1796. Travelers had to pay so that they could follow the road over the Connecticut River from New Hampshire to Vermont.

Toll roads

In C.E. 1700 people started building toll roads. A toll road is a road you have to pay to use. The people in charge then spent some of the money they made on keeping the roads repaired.

Better roads

Two British road **engineers,** Thomas Telford and John MacAdam, worked out ways to pave roads in the early 1800s. Telford's roads were stronger and lasted longer. MacAdam's roads were cheaper and still much better than unpaved roads. His system became widely used in Britain and then in other parts of the world.

A SIMILAR SYSTEM

Both Telford and MacAdam used layers to build their roads, like the Romans. Telford used several layers of stones. MacAdam used fewer layers. When rubber tires began to be used, MacAdam used tar to stick the stones on the top layer together.

Roads in the 1860s had much less traffic on them than the roads of today.

Pulled by Horses

From earliest times to about c.e. 1900, vehicles and the roads they traveled on changed, often for the better. Animals provided pulling power for carts or **coaches.** The only other ways to travel by road were to walk, to ride animals, or to be carried in special chairs by servants.

American settlers heading west in the 1800s often used oxen to pull their big wagons. Oxen were slower than horses, but they could pull four times as much weight.

Small, light coaches pulled by one or two horses were most useful in towns. On longer journeys, people used bigger coaches, pulled by more horses. On these "stagecoach" journeys, the coaches changed horses at regular stops.

This London street, painted in 1836, shows both stagecoaches and private coaches.

Coaching boom

Toll roads made travel faster and easier. Places to stay, eat, and change horses were built along the routes. Tired horses could be fed and rested. In 1740 it took 35 hours to get from London to Bath by coach. By 1820 the same journey took 12 hours.

COACH JOURNEYS

Coach travel was uncomfortable. Passengers who traveled inside were squashed together. Passengers who traveled outside, which was cheaper, were rained on, splashed with mud, or covered in dust. Everyone was bounced around.

First Cars

In 1781 a British **engineer,** James Watt, made an engine that used steam from boiling water to turn a wheel around.

Steam machines

Steam was used to drive many machines. There was even a design for a steam airplane, but it was far too heavy to get off the ground. There were many **designs** for steam carriages. They worked, but they were loud and slow.

When the first steam carriage was built, a lot of newspaper cartoons made fun of them.

Gasoline, please

From the 1860s onward, there were many **inventors** in the United States and Europe who were trying to be the first to make a gas-driven car. In 1886 Karl Benz made a three wheel car in Germany that went up to 8 miles (13 kilometers) per hour. By 1900 cars were reaching speeds of 30 miles (48 kilometers) per hour.

THE FIRST CAR

The first car with a modern design was built in France by Emile Levassor and Rene Panhard in 1891. It had a gas engine at the front, four wheels, gears, and a steering wheel.

By the early 1900s there were all types of cars and drivers on the roads.

Early Car Journeys

The first cars were expensive. Early car owners often had trouble finding a garage to store their car. They carried a spare can of gasoline, but were still likely to run out miles from a gas station. When cars broke down, drivers had to fix them themselves, or get them pushed to the nearest **blacksmith,** who would try to fix them.

Lots of cartoons made fun of how little car owners understood their new cars.

SPEED!

The following are road speeds for different vehicles, from 1700 to 1900:

- 1700 **Coach** 5 miles (8 kilometers) per hour
- 1836 Coach 9 miles (14.5 kilometers) per hour
- 1900 Horse-drawn bus 11 miles (18 kilometers) per hour
- 1900 Car 30 miles (48 kilometers) per hour.

A thrilling ride

Driving at speeds of 30 miles (48 kilometers) per hour might have been exciting, but it was also very uncomfortable. Cars were open to the weather. Drivers and passengers had to wrap themselves up well. Mud and dust were more of a problem for drivers than for walkers or horse riders, because the higher speed threw up more of both. Many motorists wore goggles to protect their eyes.

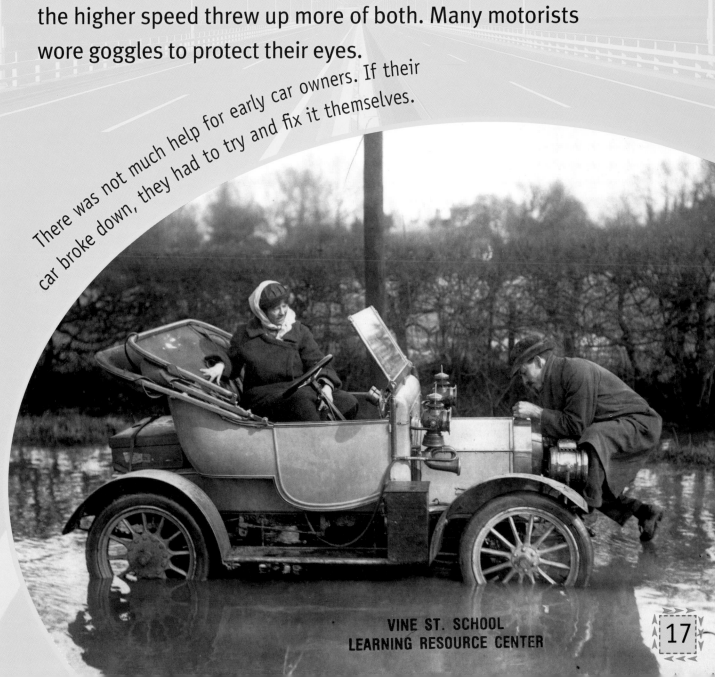

There was not much help for early car owners. If their car broke down, they had to try and fix it themselves.

Mass Production

In early car factories, each worker made a whole car. **Mass production** gave each worker one small job on each car. Cars were made faster and sold for less. In 1903 Ransom E. Olds made nearly 100 cars a week in this way. It was another American however, Henry Ford, who made mass production really work.

HENRY FORD

Henry Ford used mass production methods and conveyor belts to speed construction of his cars up. In 1913 his Ford Model T was the first car to be completely mass-produced. His factory could make 1,000 cars a day.

Rules needed!

Before mass production, any adult could buy and drive a car, without a test or a license. Most countries had a speed limit, which drivers often ignored. Roads had a white dividing line, to separate cars going in different directions. There were no rules about what to do at **intersections.**

Lights and meters

In 1914 the first set of electric traffic lights was used in the United States. It had just two lights, red and green. Parking meters were introduced in 1935. Britain had lights in 1927 and meters in 1958. Parking meters arrived in Australia in 1955.

In the United States and Australia there are many places where the road is straight and empty for miles on end.

▶▶▶▶▶▶▶▶▶

Public Transportation

People who could not afford their own vehicle had to walk or travel on public transportation. The first **public transportation** service was a horse-drawn bus service in Paris in 1662. It was not until the 1800s that many cities and towns began to have public transportation systems. Streetcars were buses pulled along rails in the road. They were used in many cities, too.

An artist painted a British Prime Minister, Gladstone, in this bus to show that people of all kinds used public transportation.

ALL SORTS OF PEOPLE

Public transportation changed the way that people lived and worked. They could travel farther to work and to shop, or have a day out. All kinds of people were crowded together on buses and streetcars.

Gasoline power

Once cars were **invented** the gas driven bus followed. The first service in the United States began in 1905, in New York City. By 1914 there were hardly any horse-drawn bus services left in the country. Buses allowed people to move around cities and towns, and from town to town. As well as normal bus services, some companies hired out buses for people who wanted to take large groups on trips.

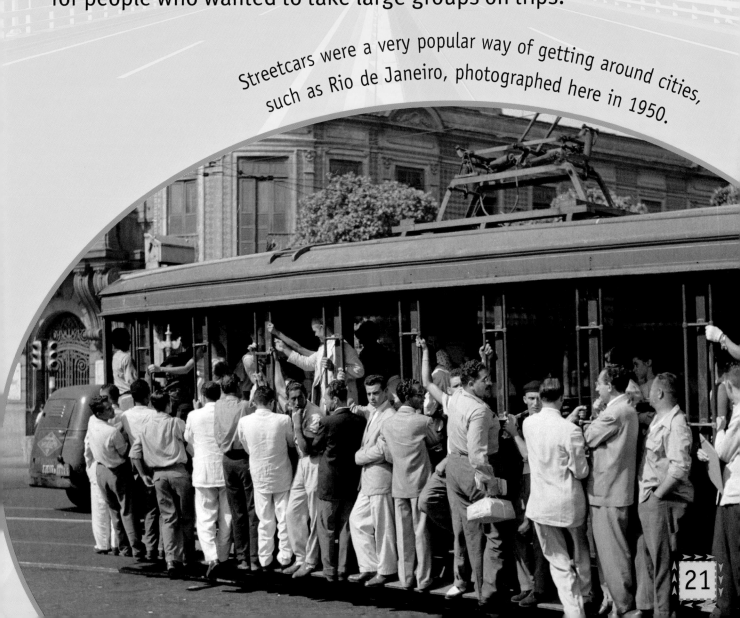

Streetcars were a very popular way of getting around cities, such as Rio de Janeiro, photographed here in 1950.

Road Revolution

After 1950 the number of cars made and sold went up rapidly. Governments built new road systems to cope. The first big roads to deal with heavy traffic were the *autobahns* built in Germany in the 1930s.

In the 1950s there were many advertisements encouraging families to buy their own car.

First choice

There were many reasons why people wanted cars. Car drivers went where they wanted, when they wanted. Train users had to fit in with train routes and timetables. The money collected from the sale of train tickets had to pay for all the costs of running the railroads. So train travel could be expensive. Car users were not usually charged to use roads, unless they were on a toll road.

Cars rule

Modern towns and cities are built, and older parts are re-built, to suit car users. Large stores and all kinds of workplaces can often only be reached easily by car. Using **public transportation** people often need to go into town and then out of it in a different direction to reach places such as airports.

Shopping at out-of-town stores is much easier for people who own cars.

STRANDED!

People who do not drive or own a car have to rely on buses, trains, or taxis to get to places like out-of-town stores. Often this can be expensive and difficult. This pushes people toward owning a car.

Trucks

Goods are moved around by road, too. For hundreds of years, goods were carried in carts over unpaved roads. Heavy carts got stuck in the mud in bad weather. Waterways and railroads were both better choices than roads for transporting heavy goods. Then the gasoline **engine** was **invented.**

Big trucks find it hard to get through narrow streets or alleys in towns or some cities.

Better roads

At first trucks with gas engines were just a useful way to move goods to places that waterways and railroads did not reach. As roads improved, trucks became a faster, cheaper way of moving goods around.

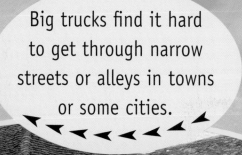

Bigger and better

Truck makers made trucks bigger and bigger. The more goods a truck could carry the better. Soon, trucks were made from more than one container with a join in the middle to go around corners and bends in the road. Refrigerated trucks were developed, to carry very cold, or even frozen, food.

Highways sometimes have truck stops, where drivers can eat, wash, and sleep.

TRUCK DRIVERS

Truck drivers spend a lot of time on the road, going from place to place. They live in the driving cab of their truck. In some countries, drivers talk to each other on radios in their cabs.

Different Worlds

Road use is very different around the world. Some countries are crammed with large, multi-lane highways. They are often crowded with traffic. Many big cities have so many cars pumping out exhaust fumes that there is a high level of **pollution.** In other countries there are fewer big roads and many unpaved ones. Far fewer people own cars.

The main roads in the city of Bejing, China, are very crowded.

MAKING CARS

The number of cars made worldwide:

- 1900   9,000
- 1950   10,500,000
- 1970   29,700,000
- 1993   36,000,000

Big differences

There are big differences in road use in the same country, too. This is especially true of big countries with large areas of countryside. In big cities in China, such as Beijing or Shanghai, there are lots of cars and many big, paved roads. The roads are not yet as crowded as in cities in the United States, but they are getting busier. In the countryside, on the other hand, few villagers own or use cars. They walk or ride bikes.

In the Chinese countryside many roads are still unpaved and most people walk or use bikes

Roads In the Future

Roads in many parts of the world are now overcrowded and dangerous. The vehicles on them cause a lot of **pollution.** The worst traffic jams, especially in cities, are caused by people going to work and coming home again. These times of the day are called "rush hours."

In cities where traffic is normally busy like this, it would not take much more traffic to bring everything to a standstill.

GRIDLOCK

It is at rush hours that people worry most about **gridlock.** This is when traffic jams up in every street so that it becomes impossible for anyone to move.

Fewer cars?

Some people who work in the same place travel to work together, to save money and to cut down the number of cars on the road. Better **public transportation** could cut these numbers even more.

Cleaner fuels

If people changed fuels, there would be less pollution. Cars can run on fuels other than gasoline. Electricity is a source of power that can run streetcars and trains and could run cars, too. In 1847 Moses Farmer **invented** the first electric car. It was not until the 1990s that electric cars and buses were used.

This car is powered by electricity.

Find Out for Yourself

You can find out more about the history of road travel by talking to adults about how travel has changed during their lifetimes. Your local library will have books about this, too. You will find the answers to many of your questions in this book, but you can also use other books and the Internet.

Books to read

Graham, Ian. *Built for Speed: Motorcycles*. Chicago: Raintree, 1998.

Parker, Vic. *Speedy Machines: Cars*. London: Belitha Press, 1999.

Using the Internet

Explore the Internet to find out more about road travel. Websites can change, so if one of the links below no longer works, don't worry. Use a search engine, such as www.yahooligans.com or www.internet4kids.com, and type in keywords such as "roads," "*autobahn*," and "cars."

Websites

www-tech.mit.edu/Subway/Archives/Project.html
Check out this historical site about New York City's first subway stations, which includes photos.

www.hfmgv.org
Visit the Henry Ford website to find out more about him and the history of car production.

Glossary

blacksmith person who mends tools and puts metal shoes on horses

chariot platform on wheels, pulled by a horse or horses

coach four-wheeled vehicle for road travel, pulled by horses

design plan or idea for something

empire all the lands controlled by one country

engine machine that uses fuel to make something work

engineer person involved in the designing and making of machines

goods things that are made, bought, and sold

gridlock when a set of roads in a town or city become so full of traffic that the traffic cannot move

intersection place where two or more roads join

invent to make or discover something for the first time

mass production making a lot of things that are all the same, all at once

Mesopotamia ancient name for part of modern Iraq

pollution causing damage to the natural world, making it dirty, messy, and often dangerous for living things

public transportation vehicles that everyone can use, once they have paid a fare

settler person who moves from one place to go and live in another

sleigh platform with strips of wood called "runners" along each side to make it easier to pull

travois wooden frame that can be loaded with baggage and pulled by a person, dog, or horse

Index